Our Favorite
Gingerbread
Recipes

Copyright 2022, Gooseberry Patch

Had I but a penny in the world,
thou shouldst have it for gingerbread.

−Shakespeare

Warm Country Gingerbread Waffles

Makes nine 4-inch waffles

2 c. all-purpose flour
1 t. cinnamon
1/2 t. ground ginger
1/2 t. salt
1 c. molasses
1/2 c. butter

1-1/2 t. baking soda
1 c. buttermilk
1 egg, beaten
Garnish: brown sugar, powdered
   sugar, hot maple syrup,
   raspberries

Combine flour, cinnamon, ginger and salt in a large bowl; set aside.
Cook molasses and butter in a saucepan over low heat until butter melts.
Remove from heat; stir in baking soda. Add buttermilk and egg; fold in
flour mixture. Ladle batter by 1/4 cupfuls onto a preheated greased waffle
iron; cook according to manufacturer's instructions. Garnish as desired.

Mix up some figgy butter to serve with waffles, pancakes and scones. In a bowl, combine one cup softened butter with one cup fig preserves, 1/2 teaspoon vanilla extract and 1/8 teaspoon nutmeg. Mix well. Transfer to a sheet of parchment paper, roll into a log and chill for at least one hour. To serve, simply slice off what you need.

Gingerbread Pancakes

Makes 8 to 10 servings

3/4 c. milk
1/2 c. strong brewed coffee,
   slightly cooled
1 egg, beaten
1-1/2 c. all-purpose flour
1 t. baking powder

1/4 t. salt
2 t. ground ginger
1 t. cinnamon
1/2 t. allspice
Garnish: maple syrup or
   powdered sugar

In a large bowl, combine all ingredients except garnish. Beat with an electric mixer on medium speed for about 30 seconds, until well combined. If batter is too runny, add a little more flour; if it is too dry, add a little more milk. Place greased metal cookie cutters onto a hot griddle over medium heat; slowly pour batter into cutters. (For plain pancakes, pour batter onto griddle by 1/4 cupfuls. Continue as directed.) Cook on first side about 10 minutes. Turn over pancakes and cutters; cook on other side for about 5 minutes. Carefully remove pancakes from cookie cutters. Serve with maple syrup or powdered sugar.

The air is brisk and the leaves are turning...it's autumn!
Invite family & friends to a cozy brunch, then take everyone
to a nearby park for a leaf hike. It's a wonderful time
for food and fun.

Perfectly Pumpkin Pancakes   *Makes 8 to 10 pancakes*

3 c. whole-wheat flour
2 T. brown sugar, packed
2 t. baking soda
3/4 t. kosher salt
1 t. cinnamon

1/8 t. ground ginger
15-oz. can pumpkin
2 c. buttermilk
1/2 c. milk
3 eggs, beaten

In a large bowl, stir together flour, brown sugar, baking soda, salt and spices. Add remaining ingredients and stir until just moistened. Let stand for several minutes to allow batter to rise. Pour batter by 1/4 cupfuls onto a hot buttered griddle over medium heat. When edges are golden, turn and cook other side. Pancakes will be very thick and may need to be turned a third time to make sure the centers are done.

It is threads, hundreds of tiny threads...which sew people together through the years.

–Simone Signoret

Sweet Apricot Coffee Cake

Makes 9 servings

2 c. crispy rice cereal, crushed
3/4 c. plus 3 T. sugar, divided
1/8 t. ground ginger
1/2 c. margarine, softened
  and divided
1-1/2 c. all-purpose flour

2 t. baking powder
1/2 t. salt
1 egg, beaten
17-oz. can apricot halves,
  chopped, drained and
1/2 c. syrup reserved

Mix together cereal, 3 tablespoons sugar, ginger and 1/4 cup margarine. Blend until crumbly; set aside for topping. In another bowl, stir together flour, baking powder and salt; set aside. In a large bowl, beat remaining margarine and sugar until well blended; add egg and beat well. Stir in reserved apricot syrup. Add flour mixture, blending well. Spread into a greased 8"x8" baking pan; spoon 3/4 cup chopped apricots evenly over batter. Sprinkle with reserved topping and remaining apricots. Bake at 350 degrees for 45 minutes, or until cake begins to pull away from sides of pan.

Mix & match! Lemon and chocolate sauces
are yummy with gingerbread cakes,
waffles and pancakes.

Spicy Pumpkin Waffles

Makes 4 large waffles or 8 pancakes

1-1/3 c. whole-wheat pastry flour
2 T. plus 2 t. sugar
2 t. baking soda
1/8 t. salt
2 t. cinnamon
1 t. nutmeg

1 t. ground ginger
4 egg whites, beaten
1 c. canned pumpkin
1 c. low-fat buttermilk
Garnish: maple syrup
Optional: toasted pumpkin seeds

In a small bowl, stir together flour, sugar, baking soda, salt and spices; set aside. In a separate bowl, whisk together egg whites, pumpkin and buttermilk. Add to flour mixture; stir just to combine. Heat a waffle iron until hot; spray with non-stick vegetable spray. Add batter to waffle iron by 1/2 cupfuls; bake according to manufacturer's instructions. Repeat with remaining batter. Serve waffles topped with maple syrup; sprinkle with pumpkin seeds, if desired.

Pour pancake batter into holiday-shaped cookie cutters...
sure to make little ones giggle! Christmas trees, snowmen
and bells are all sweet. Remember to coat the inside of
each cutter with non-stick vegetable spray and place a clip
clothespin on the side for ease in turning the pancake.

Mrs. Claus's Gingerbread Pancakes *Makes 5 pancakes*

1-1/2 c. all-purpose flour
1 t. baking powder
1/4 t. baking soda
1/4 t. salt
1 t. cinnamon

1/2 t. ground ginger
1/4 c. molasses
1 egg, beaten
1/2 t. vanilla extract
1-1/2 c. water

In a bowl, whisk together flour, baking powder, baking soda, salt and spices; set aside. In a separate large bowl, beat molasses, egg and vanilla until smooth; whisk in water until well blended. Stir flour mixture into molasses mixture until just combined; a few lumps may remain. Heat a lightly greased griddle over medium-high heat. Pour batter onto griddle by 1/4 cupfuls; cook until bubbles form on top and edges are dry. Turn and cook until golden on the other side.

Fill a muffin tin with yummy oatmeal toppings...brown sugar,
raisins, chopped nuts and even chocolate chips. So easy
for everyone to help themselves! The muffin tin can be
wrapped in plastic for serving again another day.

Exciting Oatmeal Breakfast

5 c. milk or water
1/4 t. salt
1 t. cinnamon
1/2 t. ground ginger

1/2 t. allspice
1/4 t. nutmeg
3 c. quick-cooking oats,
    uncooked

In a large saucepan over medium heat, bring milk or water and salt to a rolling boil. Add spices and oats; stir well. Cook for one minute, stirring occasionally. Cover and remove from heat; let stand 2 to 3 minutes and serve.

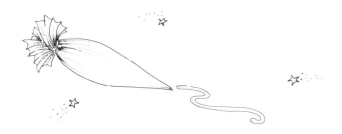

Dress up homemade scones in a snap...drizzle with melted white chocolate or powdered sugar icing.

Ginger Scones

Makes 8 scones

2-3/4 c. all-purpose flour
2 t. baking powder
1/2 t. salt
1/2 c. sugar

3/4 c. butter
1/3 c. crystallized ginger,
    chopped
1 c. milk

In a large bowl, combine flour, baking powder, salt and sugar; cut butter into flour mixture with a pastry blender until crumbly. Stir in ginger. Add milk, stirring just until mixture is moistened. Turn dough out onto a lightly floured surface and knead 10 to 15 times. Pat or roll dough to 3/4-inch thickness; shape into a round and cut dough into 8 wedges. Place wedges on a lightly greased baking sheet. Bake at 400 degrees for 18 to 22 minutes, until scones are very lightly golden. Cool slightly on a wire rack.

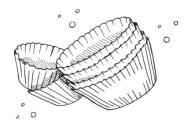

If you love freshly baked muffins, pick up a set of reusable silicone baking cups. They come in lots of bright kid-friendly colors and are also handy for other purposes like serving mini portions of fruit, nuts or chips.

My Mom's Muffin Doughnuts

Makes one dozen

2 c. all-purpose flour
1 T. baking powder
1/2 t. salt
1/2 t. nutmeg
1/2 c. plus 1/2 t. butter, divided
1-1/2 c. sugar, divided

1 egg, beaten
3/4 c. milk
3/4 c. semi-sweet chocolate chips
1/2 c. chopped pecans
2 t. cinnamon

In a large bowl, combine flour, baking powder, salt, nutmeg, 1/2 teaspoon butter, 1/2 cup sugar, egg and milk; stir well. Fold in chocolate chips and pecans. Fill 12 greased muffin cups 2/3 full. Bake at 350 degrees for 20 minutes. Remove immediately from pan. Melt remaining butter; combine remaining sugar and cinnamon. Roll muffins in melted butter, then coat with sugar and cinnamon mixture.

What a wonderful way to wake up
in the morning...with a creamy cup of Chai Tea!

Chai Tea

1 c. non-fat dry milk powder
1 c. powdered non-dairy creamer
1/2 c. sugar
2 t. ground ginger

1 t. ground cloves
1 t. ground cardamom
hot brewed black tea

In a large bowl, combine all ingredients except tea; mix well. Store mixture in a covered container. To serve, add 2 tablespoons of mixture to one cup of brewed tea.

Take time to invite a girlfriend over for afternoon tea.
Serve freshly baked cookies with a steamy pot of
Orange-Ginger Spice Tea and spend time just catching up.

Orange-Ginger Spice Tea

Makes 4 servings

2 c. water
4 thin slices fresh ginger, peeled
4-inch cinnamon stick, broken
8 whole cloves

2 tea bags
1 c. orange juice
1 T. brown sugar, packed

Combine water and spices in a saucepan; bring to a boil over high heat. Remove from heat; add tea bags and let stand for 5 minutes. Discard tea bags. Stir in orange juice and brown sugar; heat through. Strain before serving.

Always turn your slow cooker off, unplug it from the electrical outlet and allow it to cool before cleaning. The outside of the heating base may be cleaned with a soft cloth and warm soapy water.

Cinnamon-Ginger Pears

Makes 5 to 6 servings

3 c. boiling water
1 c. sugar
1/4 c. fresh ginger, peeled
   and chopped
2 4-inch cinnamon sticks

zest and juice of 2 lemons
5 to 6 pears, peeled, halved
   and cored
Garnish: vanilla Greek yogurt

Pour boiling water into a slow cooker; stir in sugar, ginger, cinnamon sticks, lemon zest and juice. Place pears into hot liquid in slow cooker. Cover and cook on low setting for 3 to 4 hours, or on high setting for one to 2 hours, until pears are tender. Discard lemon zest and cinnamon sticks. Serve pears over a serving of yogurt, drizzled with some of the sauce in slow cooker.

Peel kiwi fruit in a jiffy. Slice off both ends,
then stand the kiwi on one end and slice off
strips of peel from top to bottom.

Gingered Kiwi Fruit

Makes 4 servings

3 T. sugar
3 T. water
2 T. crystallized ginger, minced

1/4 t. vanilla extract
4 kiwi fruit, peeled and sliced
2 oranges, peeled and sliced

In a small saucepan over medium-high heat, combine sugar, water and ginger. Bring to a boil. Stirring constantly, boil until mixture reaches a light syrup consistency, about 3 minutes. Remove from heat and stir in vanilla; cool slightly. In a dessert dish, combine fruit slices and ginger syrup; stir gently until well mixed. Cover and refrigerate until well chilled, about 2 hours.

Share your homemade goodies with a friend. Wrap muffins
or scones in a tea towel and tuck them into a basket
along with a jar of jam. A sweet gift that says,
"I'm thinking of you!"

Ginger Squash Muffins

Makes one dozen

1-1/2 c. all-purpose flour
1/3 c. whole-wheat flour
1/3 c. sugar
1/4 c. brown sugar, packed
2-1/2 t. baking powder
1-1/2 t. cinnamon
1 t. ground ginger

1/2 t. salt
1 c. butternut squash, cooked
   and mashed
2 eggs, beaten
1 t. vanilla extract
1/3 c. oil
1/4 c. pecans, finely chopped

In a large bowl, combine flours, sugars, baking powder, spices and salt.
Mix well and set aside. In another bowl, combine squash, eggs, vanilla
and oil; stir until mixed well. Add to flour mixture and stir just until
combined. Fold in pecans. Spoon batter into 12 greased muffin cups,
filling 2/3 full. Bake at 375 degrees for 18 minutes, or until a toothpick
inserted in the center tests done. Cool on a wire rack before serving.

Try this delicious berry & honey spread on warm biscuits.
Combine one pint stemmed strawberries, one tablespoon lemon
juice and 1/2 cup honey in a blender until smooth. Pour into
a saucepan and simmer over low heat 20 minutes,
stirring occasionally. Makes 1-1/2 cups.

Gingerbread Muffins

Makes 2 dozen

2 c. all-purpose flour
1 t. baking powder
1/2 t. baking soda
1/2 t. salt
2 t. ground ginger
1-1/2 t. cinnamon
2 eggs, beaten

1/2 c. canola oil
1/4 c. molasses
1/4 c. plain Greek yogurt
1/4 c. brown sugar, packed
1/4 c. sugar
2 t. vanilla extract

In a bowl, mix together flour, baking powder, baking soda, salt and spices; set aside. In a separate large bowl, whisk together eggs, oil, molasses, yogurt, sugars and vanilla. Add flour mixture slowly to egg mixture; mix together until well blended. Pour batter into 24 paper-lined muffin pans, filling 2/3 full. Bake at 350 degrees for 25 to 30 minutes. Cool for no more than 5 minutes; remove muffins from pan and cool completely. Spoon Frosting into a pastry bag; decorate cooled muffins as desired.

Frosting:

1 c. powdered sugar   2 T. milk

Mix together powdered sugar and milk until blended, adding more or less milk to desired consistency.

Use a holiday tea towel to wrap up a loaf of fresh-baked quick bread. The wrapping will be a lasting gift too!

Ginger-Carrot Bread

Makes 2 loaves

3 c. all-purpose flour
2 t. cinnamon
1-1/2 t. ground ginger
1/4 t. baking powder
1 t. baking soda
2/3 c. crystallized ginger,
   finely diced

3 eggs
1 c. canola oil
1-3/4 c. sugar
2 t. vanilla extract
1 c. carrots, peeled and grated
1 c. zucchini, yellow or pattypan
   squash, grated

In a bowl, sift together flour, spices, baking powder and baking soda. Stir in crystallized ginger; set aside. In a separate large bowl, with an electric mixer on medium speed, beat eggs until light and foamy, about 2 minutes. Add oil, sugar and vanilla; beat until sugar dissolves. Add carrots and squash; mix gently until combined. Add flour mixture to egg mixture; stir gently. Coat two, 8-1/2"x4-1/2" loaf pans with non-stick vegetable spray. Spoon batter into pans. Bake at 325 degrees for about one hour, until firm and a toothpick tests clean. Cool loaves in pans on a wire rack for 15 minutes. Remove from pans; cool completely on rack.

Molasses is used in many gingerbread recipes.
Unless specified, you can use dark molasses for
full flavor or light molasses for a milder taste.

Gingerbread Biscuits

Makes 2 dozen

5 c. all-purpose flour, divided
1 t. baking soda
1/2 t. salt
1 t. cinnamon
1 t. ground ginger
1/4 t. ground cloves

1/2 c. margarine, softened
1/2 c. sugar
1 egg, beaten
3/4 c. molasses
1 c. buttermilk

In a bowl, sift together 2-1/4 cups flour, baking soda, salt and spices; set aside. In a separate large bowl, blend margarine, sugar and egg. Add flour mixture and mix well; stir in molasses and buttermilk. Stir in enough of remaining flour to make a stiff dough. Cover and refrigerate for 8 hours or overnight. On a floured surface, roll out dough to 1/8-inch thick; cut out with a biscuit cutter. Place on lightly greased baking sheets. Bake at 350 degrees for 8 to 12 minutes.

Heat limes or lemons in the microwave for 30 seconds before squeezing...you'll get twice the juice!

Ginger Thai Wings

2-1/4 lbs. chicken wings,
   separated if desired
3/4 c. water, divided
1 T. lime juice
3/4 t. ground ginger, divided

1/2 c. creamy peanut butter
2 T. soy sauce
2 cloves garlic, minced
1/4 t. red pepper flakes

Place wings in a slow cooker. Add 1/4 cup water, lime juice and 1/4 teaspoon ginger to wings; stir to coat well. Cover and cook on low setting for 5 to 6 hours. Meanwhile, whisk together peanut butter, remaining water, remaining ginger and other ingredients in a small saucepan over medium heat. Cook, whisking constantly, until mixture is smooth. Remove wings to a large bowl. Drizzle peanut sauce over wings; toss to coat well and serve.

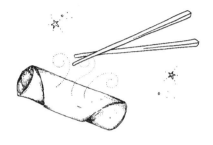

So fun with an Asian dinner! Place a 6"x6" tile
next to each guest's place and rest chopsticks
on top...just be sure to have forks available too!

Golden Fortune Egg Rolls

Makes 18 to 20 servings

1 lb. ground pork sausage,
  browned and drained
2 16-oz. pkgs. coleslaw mix
3 T. fresh ginger, peeled and
  minced
3 T. garlic, finely chopped

1 t. salt
1 T. pepper
18 to 20 egg roll wrappers
oil for deep frying
Garnish: spicy mustard,
  sweet-and-sour sauce

In a large bowl, combine browned sausage, coleslaw mix, ginger, garlic, salt and pepper; mix well. Transfer mixture to a colander; let drain for 15 minutes. Assemble egg rolls according to package directions, using 1/3 cup sausage mixture for each; set aside. Heat 3 inches oil to 375 degrees in a wok, Dutch oven or deep fryer. Fry egg rolls 3 to 4 at a time until golden, about 3 minutes. Drain on paper towels. Serve with sauces for dipping.

Primitive-style wooden cutting boards in fun shapes
like pigs, fish or roosters can often be found at
tag sales. Put them to use as whimsical
party snack servers.

Ginger Cocktail Sausages

Makes about 4 dozen

2 egg yolks
1 lb. ground pork sausage
1/2 c. dill pickle, chopped

1 t. ground ginger
2 T. all-purpose flour

Beat egg yolks in a large bowl. Add sausage, pickle and ginger, blending well. Cover and chill for 2 to 3 hours. Form into small sausages, about one inch long and 1/2-inch in diameter, or to desired size. Roll each sausage in flour. Cook sausages in a skillet over medium heat, turning occasionally until lightly browned and cooked through. Serve warm.

Set up tables in different areas of the house
so guests have room to mingle as they enjoy
yummy finger foods and beverages. Your party
is sure to be a festive success!

Simply Scrumptious Sticky Wings

Makes 8 servings

3/4 c. dark brown sugar, packed
   and divided
1/4 c. soy sauce, divided
4 cloves garlic, minced
2 T. fresh ginger, minced
1/2 t. cayenne pepper, divided

4 lbs. chicken wings, separated
   if desired
salt and pepper to taste
1/4 c. water
1/4 c. tomato paste

In a slow cooker, combine 1/4 cup brown sugar, one tablespoon soy sauce, garlic, ginger and 1/4 teaspoon cayenne pepper. Season chicken wings with salt and pepper; add to sugar mixture. Toss wings to coat well. Cover and cook on low setting for 4 to 5 hours, until chicken is tender and no longer pink in the center. Remove wings to a rack on an aluminum foil-lined baking sheet; set aside. In a bowl, combine remaining brown sugar, soy sauce and cayenne pepper, water and tomato paste; mix well. Brush wings with half of sauce. Broil wings until crisp on one side, about 10 minutes. Turn wings and brush with remaining sauce; broil until crisp on the other side, about 5 minutes.

Host a family reunion this fall...the weather is almost always picture-perfect! When sending invitations, be sure to encourage everyone to bring photos, recipes, videos, scrapbooks and anything that inspires memories.

Maple-Topped Sweet Potato Skins

Serves 12

6 large sweet potatoes
1/2 c. cream cheese, softened
1/4 c. sour cream
2 t. cinnamon, divided
2 t. nutmeg, divided
2 t. ground ginger, divided

2 c. chopped walnuts or pecans
3 T. butter, softened
1/4 c. brown sugar, packed
Garnish: maple syrup, apple slices,
  additional nuts

Pierce potatoes with a fork. Bake at 400 degrees or microwave on high setting until tender; cool. Slice potatoes in half lengthwise; scoop out baked insides, keeping skins intact. Mash baked potato in a bowl until smooth; add cream cheese, sour cream and one teaspoon each of spices. Mix well and spoon into potato skins. Mix nuts, butter, brown sugar and remaining spices; sprinkle over top. Place potato skins on an ungreased baking sheet; bake at 400 degrees for 15 minutes. Drizzle with warm syrup; garnish as desired.

For small town games, there isn't always lots of room for a big tailgating party, so have a cookout before! Everyone can get in the spirit, enjoy some tasty food and walk to the game together.

Sesame Beef Strips

1 T. toasted sesame seed, crushed
6 T. soy sauce
2 T. sugar
1 green onion, sliced
1 t. fresh ginger, peeled
    and minced

2 cloves garlic, minced
1/8 t. pepper
1 T. oil
1-1/2 lbs. boneless beef, cut into
    1/8-inch strips

In a large bowl, whisk together all ingredients except oil and beef strips; fold in beef strips. Cover and refrigerate for 2 hours. Heat oil in a large skillet; add beef strips, discarding marinade. Sauté until browned; arrange on a platter. Serve using toothpicks.

Add a little flair to your party punch! Scoop a quart of lemon or raspberry sherbet into 8 balls and freeze until serving time. To serve, place each ball in a frosted stemmed glass. Carefully pour 1/2 cup chilled punch over the sherbet and garnish with a sprig of fresh mint.

Refreshing Mint Punch

Serves 10 to 12

2 c. fresh mint leaves, packed
2 c. water
1 qt. ginger ale, chilled

12-oz. can frozen lemonade
concentrate, thawed

Bring mint and water to boil; bruise mint with a potato masher. Cover and refrigerate overnight. To serve, strain and discard solids. Add ginger ale, lemonade and 3 lemonade cans of cold water to mint mixture; mix well and serve.

Pecans and almonds would make a nice
alternative to the walnuts...or mix them
all together!

Sugared Walnuts

Makes 16 servings

1 lb. walnut halves
1/2 c. butter, melted
1/2 c. powdered sugar

1-1/2 t. cinnamon
1/4 t. ground cloves
1/4 t. ground ginger

Preheat a slow cooker on high setting for 15 minutes. Add walnuts and butter, stirring to mix well. Add powdered sugar; mix until coated evenly. Cover and cook on high setting for 15 minutes. Reduce heat to low setting. Cook, uncovered, stirring occasionally, for 2 to 3 hours, or until nuts are coated with a crisp glaze. Transfer nuts to a serving bowl. Combine spices in a small bowl and sprinkle over nuts, stirring to coat evenly. Cool before serving. Store in an airtight container.

Hand deliver edible Christmas cards this year.
Just cut gingerbread into postcard-size pieces,
bake and pipe on holiday wishes with royal icing...
top off with gumdrops and candy canes!

Ginger Pennies

Makes 10 to 12 dozen

1 c. brown sugar, packed
1 egg, beaten
1/4 c. blackstrap molasses
3/4 c. butter, softened
1-1/2 c. all-purpose flour

1/2 t. baking soda
1/4 t. salt
3/4 t. ground ginger
3/4 t. cinnamon
1/2 t. ground cloves

Blend brown sugar, egg, molasses and butter in a large bowl; set aside.
In another bowl, mix together flour, baking soda, salt and spices; beat
into brown sugar mixture. Spoon batter into a gallon-size plastic zipping
bag; snip off a small corner. Pipe small dots of batter (about 1/8 teaspoon
or a 1-1/2 inch mound) onto greased baking sheets, one inch apart. Bake
at 325 degrees for 3 minutes. Immediately remove from baking sheets
onto wire racks; let cool. May be stored in an airtight container for
several months.

Search Grandma's recipe box for that extra-special
cookie you remember...and then bake some to share
with the whole family. If you don't have her recipe
box, maybe you'll spot a similar recipe in a
Gooseberry Patch cookbook!

Cinnamon & Ginger Nuts

Makes 3 cups

3 c. mixed nuts
1 egg white
1 T. orange juice
2/3 c. sugar

1 t. cinnamon
1/2 t. ground ginger
1/2 t. allspice
1/4 t. salt

Place nuts in a large mixing bowl; set aside. Whisk egg white and orange juice together until frothy; mix in remaining ingredients. Pour over nuts; mix thoroughly. Spread coated nuts onto an aluminum foil-lined baking sheet. Bake at 275 degrees for 45 minutes, stirring every 15 minutes. Cool; store in an airtight container.

Carrying a salad to a school potluck or a family picnic?
Mix it up in a plastic zipping bag instead of a bowl, seal and
set it on ice in a picnic cooler. No more worries about
leaks or spills!

Gingered Chicken & Fruit Salad

Makes 8 servings

1-1/2 to 2 c. mayonnaise
2 T. ground ginger
2 c. cooked chicken breast, cubed
1 c. green and/or red seedless
   grapes, halved lengthwise
1 c. pineapple chunks

3 Red Delicious apples, peeled,
   cored and diced
3 Granny Smith apples, peeled,
   cored and diced
1/2 c. slivered almonds

In a small bowl, stir together mayonnaise and ginger; set aside. Combine remaining ingredients in a large bowl. Add mayonnaise mixture; toss lightly until well blended and coated. Cover and chill until serving time.

Roasted cherry tomatoes make a delightful garnish for
dinner plates and salads...small clusters of tomatoes can
even be left on the stem. Place tomatoes in a small casserole
dish and drizzle with olive oil. Bake at 450 degrees for
15 minutes, or until soft and slightly wrinkled.
Serve warm or chilled.

Gingered Shrimp & Snow Peas

Serves 4

3/4 lb. snow peas, trimmed
1-1/4 lbs. medium shrimp, cleaned
6 radishes, thinly sliced
4 green onions, thinly sliced
1/3 c. vinegar
1 T. canola oil

1 T. toasted sesame oil
1 T. fresh ginger, peeled
    and grated
salt to taste
2 T. toasted sesame seed

Place a steamer basket in a large saucepan; fill pan with water and bring to a boil. Add snow peas; cover and cook for 2 minutes. Remove basket, reserving boiling water in saucepan; transfer peas to a bowl of ice water to cool. Drain peas and pat dry; cut on the diagonal into 1/2-inch pieces. Add shrimp directly to boiling water; return to a boil and cook for 2 minutes. Drain shrimp; plunge into a bowl of ice water. Drain and pat dry; slice shrimp in half lengthwise. In a large bowl, toss shrimp, peas, radishes and onions together. In a small bowl, whisk together vinegar, oils and ginger; add salt to taste. Drizzle vinegar mixture over salad; toss salad and top with sesame seed.

Greet visitors with a charming homespun wreath on the door. Simply tear checked homespun fabric in golds and browns into strips and tie onto a grapevine wreath.

Honey-Ginger Wild Rice Salad

3 c. cooked wild rice
1 to 2 bunches green onions,
    sliced
1 c. sweetened dried cranberries

1 c. red pepper, diced
1/2 c. salted roasted sunflower
    kernels
3/4 c. pine nuts

Combine all ingredients except pine nuts in a large salad bowl; toss to mix and set aside. Toast pine nuts in a dry skillet over medium-high heat, stirring until fragrant. Cool slightly and add to salad. Drizzle with Honey-Ginger Dressing; stir thoroughly to combine. Cover and refrigerate until serving time.

Honey-Ginger Dressing:

2 T. frozen orange juice
    concentrate
2 T. honey
2 T. toasted sesame oil

1 T. rice vinegar
1 T. soy sauce
1 to 2 T. fresh ginger, peeled
    and grated

Whisk together all ingredients, adding ginger to taste.

Serving juicy, fruit-filled salads outdoors can sometimes
be tricky, so why not spoon individual servings into
one-pint, wide-mouth Mason jars? Secure the lids,
and when it's serving time, friends will find the tasty
fruit salad, and the juices, stay right inside the jars!

Marsha's Cheery Cherry Salad

15-oz. can tart cherries, drained
    and juice reserved
8-1/2 oz. can crushed pineapple,
    drained and juice reserved

1/2 c. sugar
2 3-oz. pkgs. cherry gelatin mix
1-1/2 c. ginger ale
Optional: 1/2 c. chopped pecans

Pour reserved cherry and pineapple juices into a 2-cup measuring cup.
Add enough water to equal 1-3/4 cups. Pour into a small saucepan and
add sugar. Bring to a boil over medium heat. Stir in gelatin mix; remove
from heat. Add fruit and ginger ale. Pour into a large serving bowl. Cover
and chill in refrigerator until thickened, but not completely set. Stir in
pecans, if desired. Return to refrigerator until fully set.

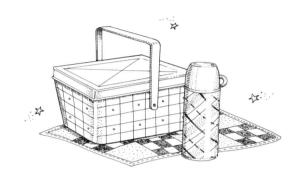

Happiness is like potato salad...
when shared with others, it's a picnic!

—Unknown

Chinese Coleslaw

9 c. napa cabbage, shredded
4 c. green cabbage, shredded
1 c. red or green pepper, sliced
1 c. snow peas

1 c. bean sprouts
5 green onions, sliced
Garnish: 2 T. toasted sesame seed

Combine vegetables in a large bowl. Drizzle with Sesame-Ginger Dressing; toss and sprinkle with sesame seed. Toss once more before serving.

Sesame-Ginger Dressing:

1 clove garlic, minced
1/8-inch-thick slice fresh ginger, peeled and minced
1/4 c. sesame seed oil or peanut oil

3 T. soy sauce
3 T. rice wine vinegar
1 t. sugar
Optional: 4 drops chili oil

Combine all ingredients in a jar with a tight-fitting lid. Secure lid and shake well to blend.

Fruity gelatin salads are yummy when topped with a dollop of creamy lemon mayonnaise. To 1/2 cup mayonnaise, add 3 tablespoons each of lemon juice, light cream and powdered sugar.

Ginger Ale Salad

Serves 8

1/2 c. boiling water
3-oz. pkg. lemon gelatin mix
1-1/3 c. ginger ale, chilled
1 c. seedless red grapes, halved

11-oz. can mandarin oranges,
  drained
11-oz. can pineapple tidbits,
  drained

In a bowl, add boiling water to gelatin mix; stir until dissolved. Stir in ginger ale; cover and chill. When gelatin begins to thicken, stir in fruit. Cover and chill 2 to 3 hours, until completely set.

Sit in front of a cozy fire and stitch up some handmade gifts for friends & family. They'll treasure a sweet little sachet filled with dried lavender, squares of felted wool for coasters, or an embroidered tea towel.

Dijon-Ginger Carrots

Makes 12 servings

12 carrots, peeled and sliced
    1/4-inch thick
1/3 c. Dijon mustard
1/2 c. brown sugar, packed

1 t. fresh ginger, peeled
    and minced
1/4 t. salt
1/8 t. pepper

Combine all ingredients in a slow cooker; stir. Cover and cook on high setting for 2 to 3 hours, until carrots are tender, stirring twice during cooking.

Keep all of your family's favorite holiday storybooks
in a basket by a cozy chair. Set aside one night as
family night to read your favorites together.

Festive Apples & Squash

4-lb. butternut squash, halved
   and seeds removed
2/3 c. butter, melted
1 c. light brown sugar, packed
3 T. all-purpose flour
1/2 t. salt

1 t. cinnamon
1/2 t. ground ginger
1/2 t. nutmeg
6 Granny Smith apples, peeled,
   cored and sliced

Peel squash and cut into 1/2-inch cubes; set aside. Combine butter, brown sugar, flour, salt and spices; mix until crumbly. Layer half of squash in an oval slow cooker. Top with half of the apple slices and half of the spice mixture. Repeat layers. Cover and cook on low setting for 6 hours, or on high setting for 3-1/2 hours, until squash and apples are tender.

If time is tight, streamline your holiday plans... just ask
your family what festive foods and traditions they
cherish the most. Then focus on tried & true activities
and free up time to try something new.

Sweet Potatoes in Baskets

Makes 6 servings

3 c. sweet potatoes, peeled, cooked
    and mashed
1/4 to 1/2 c. brown sugar, packed
2 eggs, beaten
1/2 t. lemon zest
1/2 t. salt

1/2 t. cinnamon
1/4 t. ground ginger
1/4 t. ground cloves
6 navel oranges
Garnish: marshmallows, or walnut
    or pecan halves

In a bowl, combine sweet potatoes, brown sugar, eggs, salt and spices.
Mix thoroughly and set aside. Cut tops off oranges in zig-zag style,
leaving shells intact. Scoop out orange pulp with a spoon. Fill scooped-out
orange shells with sweet potato mixture, adding some of the orange pulp if
mixture is too thick. Place oranges in an ungreased baking pan. Bake,
uncovered, at 350 degrees for 25 to 30 minutes. Top each with a
marshmallow or a nut half; return to oven for 2 minutes, or until golden.

Pick up a vintage divided serving dish or two...
they're just right for serving up a choice
of veggie sides without crowding the table.

Gingered Broccoli

Makes 6 servings

2 t. olive oil
2 T. fresh ginger, peeled
    and grated
3 cloves garlic, chopped

1 lb. fresh or frozen broccoli
    flowerets
3 T. soy sauce

Heat oil in a skillet over medium heat. Add ginger and garlic; sauté for one to 2 minutes. Add broccoli; cook to desired tenderness. Add soy sauce; cook over low heat for several more minutes to allow flavors to blend. Serve immediately.

This is my invariable advice to people:
Learn how to cook...try new recipes,
learn from your mistakes, be fearless,
and above all, have fun!

–Julia Child

Honey-Ginger Carrots

Serves 4

1 lb. carrots, peeled and sliced
1/4 t. salt
1/4 c. butter
3 T. honey

1 to 1-1/2 t. fresh ginger,
   peeled and grated
Garnish: chopped fresh parsley

Place carrots in a saucepan; add a small amount of water to just cover carrots. Sprinkle with salt. Cook over medium-high heat just until carrots are tender; drain. Remove from heat. Add butter, honey and ginger; stir until butter and honey are melted. Garnish with chopped parsley.

When chopping ingredients, be sure not to mix fresh
veggies and raw meat on the same cutting board.
Use two separate cutting boards, or wash
the cutting board well in between ingredients.
Don't place cooked food on a plate that has
had raw meat on it.

Marinated Flank Steak

Makes 6 servings

1-1/3 lb. beef flank steak
2 T. low-sodium soy sauce
2 T. honey
2 T. white vinegar
1-1/2 T. ground ginger

1-1/2 t. garlic powder
1-1/2 t. cinnamon
1-1/2 t. nutmeg
1/4 c. oil
1 onion, chopped

Using a sharp knife, make shallow cuts in steak; set aside. Mix together remaining ingredients in a large plastic zipping bag; add steak. Seal bag and refrigerate for at least 24 hours, turning several times. Remove steak from bag; discard marinade. Grill or broil steak for 5 to 10 minutes on each side, to desired doneness. Slice steak thinly on an angle to serve.

Nothing beats the taste of fresh-picked herbs and
vegetables! Even the smallest yard is sure to have
a sunny corner where you can grow sun-ripened tomatoes
and an herb or two in a wooden half-barrel. Seeds,
plants and free advice are available at the
nearest garden store.

Polynesian Ginger Spareribs

Serves 4 to 6

1/2 c. soy sauce
1/2 c. brown sugar, packed
1/2 c. green onions, chopped
1/4 c. catsup

2 cloves garlic, pressed
1 t. fresh ginger, peeled and grated
3 lbs. pork spareribs, cut into
serving-size portions

In a microwave-safe dish, mix all ingredients except spareribs. Add spareribs; turn until well coated. Drain marinade into a small saucepan; bring to a boil for 3 minutes and remove from heat. Cover ribs with plastic wrap; let stand for 10 minutes. Microwave ribs on medium-high setting for 12 to 16 minutes. Place ribs on an oiled grill over medium-high heat; brush with marinade. Grill for 8 to 10 minutes, turning and brushing once or twice with marinade.

Gas or charcoal? Every cookout chef has his or her own opinion! A good rule of thumb is charcoal for taste, gas for haste.

Lime & Ginger Grilled Salmon

Serves 4 to 6

2-lb. salmon fillet
2 T. fresh ginger, peeled
   and minced
2 T. lime zest

1/2 t. salt
1/2 t. pepper
2 T. butter, melted, or olive oil
1/2 t. lime juice

Preheat grill to medium-high heat (350 to 400 degrees). Sprinkle salmon with ginger, lime zest, salt and pepper. Combine butter or olive oil and lime juice in a small bowl; brush salmon with mixture. Grill for about 5 minutes on each side, until salmon flakes easily with a fork.

When spring cleaning time rolls around, slow-cooker dishes
make mealtime a breeze. Add all the ingredients,
turn it on and forget about it. Now, throw open the
windows and air out the quilts with no worries
about what's for dinner!

Orange & Ginger Beef Ribs

Serves 6

1/3 c. soy sauce
3 T. brown sugar, packed
3 T. white vinegar
2 cloves garlic, minced
1/2 t. chili powder

1 T. fresh ginger, peeled
  and minced
3 lbs. boneless beef short ribs
1/3 c. orange marmalade

In a large plastic zipping bag, combine all ingredients except ribs and marmalade. Add ribs to bag; turn to coat well. Refrigerate at least 2 hours to overnight. Drain ribs, reserving marinade. Place ribs in a large slow cooker. Add marmalade to reserved marinade; mix well and pour over ribs. Cover and cook on high setting for 4 hours, or on low setting for 6 to 8 hours.

Keep kitchen scissors nearby...they make short work
of snipping fresh herbs, chopping green onions or even
cutting up whole tomatoes right in the can.

Key West Citrus Chicken

Serves 4

4 boneless, skinless chicken
   breasts
salt and pepper to taste
1/3 c. orange juice

3 cloves garlic, minced
1/4 t. ground ginger
1/8 t. red pepper flakes
Garnish: orange slices

Season chicken with salt and pepper; place in a skillet sprayed with non-stick vegetable spray. Cook chicken over medium heat until tender and no longer pink, 8 to 10 minutes, turning once. Stir together orange juice, garlic, ginger and red pepper flakes in a small bowl; pour into skillet. Bring to a boil; reduce heat and simmer, uncovered, for 2 minutes. To serve, spoon pan juices over chicken; top with orange slices.

The true essentials of a feast
are only food and fun.

–Oliver Wendell Holmes, Sr.

Evelyn's Grilled Pork Loin

Serves 6 to 8

3-lb. boneless pork loin roast
1 c. soy sauce
1/2 c. sherry or apple juice
1 t. mustard

1 t. ground ginger
1/2 t. salt
1/4 t. garlic powder

Place roast in a shallow glass dish. Combine remaining ingredients in a bowl; mix well and spoon over roast. Cover and refrigerate for 2 hours to overnight. Drain marinade into a small saucepan; bring to a boil for 3 minutes. Place roast on a grill over medium-high heat, 6 to 8 inches above heat. Cover and grill for 1-1/2 to 2 hours, turning and brushing with marinade every 30 minutes. Slice roast thinly to serve.

Create a meal plan for the week, including all of
your favorite quick & easy meals...spaghetti on Monday,
chicken pot pie on Tuesday and so forth. Post it
on the fridge along with a shopping list...
making dinner will be a snap!

Simple Ginger Chicken

Serves 6 to 8

6 to 8 chicken thighs
1/2 to 1 onion, chopped
1 c. low-sodium soy sauce

1 c. water
3 T. ground ginger, or to taste
cooked rice

Combine all ingredients except rice in a Dutch oven. Bring to a boil over medium-high heat; reduce heat to low. Cover and simmer for one hour, or until chicken juices run clear. Check occasionally, adding more water as needed. May also be cooked in a slow cooker on low setting for 6 to 8 hours. Serve chicken and pan juices over cooked rice.

For casual parties, a serve-yourself
drink dispenser (or 2!) can't be beat.

Ginger-Pumpkin Soup

15-oz. can pumpkin
1 red onion, chopped
2 stalks celery, chopped
2 sweet potatoes, peeled
    and chopped
3 cloves garlic, chopped
1-inch piece fresh ginger, peeled
    and grated
4 c. vegetable broth

2 c. water
1 T. sugar
2 t. salt
1 t. turmeric
1/4 t. allspice
1/4 t. nutmeg
Garnish: whipping cream,
    chopped green onion,
    roasted pumpkin seeds

Combine pumpkin, onion, celery, sweet potatoes, garlic and ginger in a slow cooker. Stir in broth and water. Add remaining ingredients except garnish to slow cooker; mix well. Cover and cook on low setting for 8 hours. If desired, process 3/4 of the soup in a blender or with an immersion blender until smooth; return to soup in slow cooker. Drizzle servings with cream; sprinkle with green onion and pumpkin seeds.

Tender baked potatoes from your slow cooker...it's easy!
Pierce 6 baking potatoes with a fork and wrap each in
aluminum foil. Stack in a slow cooker. Cover and cook
on low setting 8 to 10 hours, or on high setting
for 2-1/2 to 4 hours.

Hearty Carrot Soup

32-oz. container sodium-free
   beef broth
2-1/2 lbs. carrots, peeled
   and sliced
1/4 c. onion, diced

2 cloves garlic, minced
2 T. brown sugar, packed
1 T. ground ginger
1/4 c. whipping cream

In a slow cooker, combine broth, carrots, onion and garlic. Cover and cook on high setting for 5 hours, or on low setting for 8 hours, until carrots break apart easily. Working in batches, transfer contents of slow cooker to a blender or food processor, or use an immersion blender in slow cooker. Process soup for about one minute, until desired consistency is reached. Stir in remaining ingredients. Serve warm.

Twisty bread sticks are a tasty go-with for soup.
Brush refrigerated bread stick dough with a little
beaten egg and dust with Italian seasoning, then
pop 'em in the oven until toasty. Yummy!

Oriental Chicken Soup

Serves 4

3 14-1/2 oz. cans chicken broth
2 c. water
1 T. fresh ginger, peeled
  and grated
1 clove garlic, slivered
1/4 to 1/2 t. red pepper flakes
8-oz. pkg. whole-wheat spaghetti,
  uncooked and divided

2 boneless, skinless chicken
  breasts, thinly sliced
1 red pepper, thinly sliced
1 c. snow peas, chopped
juice of 1 lime
2 green onions, thinly sliced
salt to taste

In a large soup pot over high heat, bring chicken broth, water, ginger, garlic and red pepper flakes to a boil. Add half of the spaghetti, reserving remainder for a future use. Reduce heat to medium; simmer until spaghetti is tender, about 6 to 8 minutes. Add chicken, pepper and snow peas; simmer until chicken is fully cooked, about 3 minutes. Stir in lime juice, green onions and salt.

Toting some homemade chicken soup to a friend who's
under the weather? Remember all the nice things
that go along with making someone feel better...
crossword puzzles, a book by a favorite author,
a box of tissues and a hot water bottle.

Cold-Chaser Chicken Soup

Makes 8 servings

2 boneless, skinless chicken
    breasts
8 c. chicken broth
1 c. onion, diced
2 stalks celery, diced
2 carrots, peeled and diced
6 cloves garlic, minced

1/2 to 1-inch piece fresh ginger,
    peeled and minced
1 T. poultry seasoning
1 t. red pepper flakes
salt and pepper to taste
1 c. favorite tri-color vegetable
    pasta, uncooked

Spray a skillet with non-stick vegetable spray. Add chicken; sauté over medium heat until no longer pink. Set chicken aside to cool; dice chicken. Meanwhile, in a soup pot over medium-high heat, bring chicken broth to a boil. Stir in vegetables, garlic, ginger and seasonings; reduce heat to low. Cover and simmer for 30 minutes, stirring occasionally. Add diced chicken; cover and simmer for another 30 minutes. Return to a boil; stir in uncooked pasta. Cook over medium-high heat just until pasta is tender.

For a fruit-studded ice ring that won't dilute your
holiday punch, arrange sliced oranges, lemons and limes
in a ring mold. Pour in a small amount of punch and
freeze until set. Add enough punch to fill mold
and freeze until solid. To turn out, dip mold carefully
in warm water.

Fireside Mulled Cider

Makes 12 servings

3 qts. apple cider
1/2 c. apple jelly
1/4 t. nutmeg
2 strips orange peel,
    4-inch by 1-inch

3 whole cloves
2 whole allspice
4-inch cinnamon stick
1/2-inch piece fresh ginger, peeled

Combine cider, jelly and nutmeg in a 4-quart slow cooker; set aside. Place remaining ingredients in a square of doubled cheesecloth. Tie with kitchen string and add to slow cooker. Cover and cook on high setting for 4 hours. Discard spice bag before serving.

For an easy frosting to decorate your Gingerbread Pinwheels, combine 2-1/2 cups powdered sugar, 3 tablespoons melted butter, 3 tablespoons milk, one teaspoon vanilla extract and one teaspoon lemon juice in a large bowl. Beat with an electric mixer on low speed until smooth. If necessary, add a few more drops of milk for desired consistency.

Gingerbread Pinwheels

Makes about 3-1/2 dozen

1/3 c. brown sugar, packed
1/3 c. shortening
2/3 c. molasses
1 egg, beaten
3 c. all-purpose flour

1 T. baking powder
1-1/2 t. ground ginger
1/2 t. salt
Optional: gumdrops

In a bowl, beat together brown sugar and shortening until light and fluffy. Beat in molasses. Add egg, beating well; set aside. In a separate large bowl, sift together flour, baking powder, ginger and salt. Add flour mixture to brown sugar mixture; mix well. Cover and refrigerate for 2 hours. Divide dough into 4 parts. On a floured surface, roll out each part to 1/4-inch thickness. Cut into 3-inch squares; place on greased baking sheets. Cut each square in from all 4 corners; fold each corner to the center to form a pinwheel. (See cover of book for finished cookie.) Bake at 350 degrees for 5 to 7 minutes, until dark golden. Cool slightly on pans; remove to wire racks to cool completely. Pipe with Frosting (recipe at left, page 102); add a gumdrop to the centers, if desired.

Ginger comes in several different forms...ground, crystallized and fresh. For best results, use the kind specified in a recipe, but in a pinch, 1/4 teaspoon ground ginger equals one tablespoon sliced fresh ginger root equals 1/4 cup minced crystallized ginger.

Grandma's Gingersnaps

Makes about 4 dozen

3/4 c. butter, softened
1 c. sugar
1 egg, beaten
1/2 c. molasses
2 T. fresh ginger, peeled
    and grated

2 c. all-purpose flour
2 t. baking soda
1/2 t. salt
1 T. cinnamon
Garnish: additional sugar

Blend butter and sugar in a large bowl; add egg and beat until fluffy.
Mix in molasses and ginger; set aside. In another bowl, combine flour,
baking soda, salt and cinnamon; stir into butter mixture. Shape dough
into one-inch balls; roll in additional sugar and arrange on lightly greased
baking sheets. Bake at 350 degrees for 10 to 12 minutes. Cool on
wire racks.

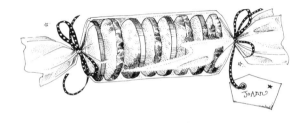

Roll stacks of cookies in clear or tinted cellophane and tie the ends with curling ribbon...pile up in a pretty basket as welcome favors for holiday visitors.

Soft Gingerbread Drop Cookies   *Makes about 6 dozen*

1 c. margarine
1-1/2 c. brown sugar, packed
2 eggs, beaten
1/2 c. molasses
1 T. ground ginger
1-1/2 c. boiling water

5 c. all-purpose flour
2 t. baking powder
1-1/2 t. baking soda
1-1/2 t. salt
1 T. cinnamon
1 c. chopped walnuts

Blend margarine and sugar in a large bowl; stir in eggs. Mix in molasses and ginger; stir in water. Combine remaining ingredients except walnuts; mix well and add to margarine mixture. Stir well; fold in walnuts. Cover and refrigerate at least 2 hours. Drop dough by teaspoonfuls onto ungreased baking sheets. Bake at 425 degrees for 10 to 12 minutes, until golden.

At holiday time, host a dessert open house for
friends & neighbors instead of an elaborate party.
Serve lots of cookies with coffee, tea and
hot cocoa...just add fun and fellowship for a
delightful no-stress afternoon!

Dipped Gingerbread Stars

Makes about 5 dozen

1 c. shortening
1 c. brown sugar, packed
3/4 c. molasses
3/4 c. buttermilk
2 eggs, beaten
4-1/2 c. all-purpose flour

1 T. ground ginger
2 t. baking soda
1 t. salt
Garnish: white and/or semi-sweet
   chocolate chips, melted

In a large bowl, blend shortening and brown sugar. Add molasses, buttermilk and eggs; stir well and set aside. In a separate bowl, mix flour, ginger, baking soda and salt. Blend flour mixture into shortening mixture. Mix well; cover and refrigerate overnight. Roll out dough 1/4-inch thick on a lightly floured surface; cut out with a star cookie cutter. Arrange on ungreased baking sheets. Bake at 400 degrees for 10 to 12 minutes. Let cool completely; dip half of each cookie into melted chocolate. Place cookies on wax paper to set.

Run! Run! As fast as you can!
You can't catch me, I'm the gingerbread man!

—Old folktale

Gingerbread Men

Makes 4 to 5 dozen

1 c. butter, softened
1 c. sugar
1 c. molasses
2 T. ground ginger
Optional: 1/4 c. crystallized ginger,
    finely chopped

1 t. baking soda
1 t. salt
5 c. all-purpose flour, divided

In a bowl, blend together butter, sugar and molasses. Stir in ginger and crystallized ginger, if using. In a large bowl, combine baking soda, salt and one cup flour; add to butter mixture. Stir in remaining flour, 1/4 cup at a time, kneading by hand as dough becomes stiff. Knead dough until well blended. Roll out onto a lightly floured surface to 1/4-inch thick. Cut out desired shapes with a cookie cutter; arrange on parchment paper-lined baking sheets. Bake at 350 degrees for 8 to 10 minutes, until golden.

Use heart, diamond, club and spade cookie cutters
to cut out Dutch Speculaas...deliver with a package of
new playing cards to your favorite bridge partner.

Dutch Speculaas

Makes about 3 dozen

3 c. all-purpose flour
1/8 t. baking powder
1/8 t. salt
1-1/2 t. cinnamon
1 t. ground cloves
1 t. ground ginger

1 c. butter
1-1/4 c. light brown sugar, packed
1 egg
1/2 c. blanched almonds,
    finely ground

In a bowl, stir together flour, baking powder, salt and spices; set aside. In a separate bowl, with an electric mixer on high speed, beat butter, brown sugar and egg until blended. Using a wooden spoon, gradually stir in flour mixture. Finish mixing with hands, if necessary; stir in almonds. Cover and chill dough for several hours. Roll out dough thinly between sheets of wax paper; cut with cookie cutters as desired. Arrange on greased baking sheets. Bake at 350 degrees for about 10 to 15 minutes, until lightly golden but not overbaked, about 10 to 15 minutes.

This Buttercream Frosting works well when making an Old-Fashioned Gingerbread Torte. Melt 1/2 cup white chocolate chips; set aside to cool. In a large mixing bowl, beat one cup softened butter until very fluffy. Add 6 to 7 cups powdered sugar and 6 to 9 tablespoons milk in small batches, beating after each addition until very fluffy. Stir in 2 teaspoons vanilla extract, 1/4 teaspoon salt and melted chocolate. Use immediately.

Old-Fashioned Gingerbread Torte   *Makes 16 servings*

3 c. all-purpose flour
3/4 t. baking soda
3/4 t. salt
1 T. ground ginger
1-1/2 t. cinnamon

1-1/2 c. light molasses
1 c. water
3/4 c. butter, softened
3/4 c. sugar
2 eggs

Stir together flour, baking soda, salt and spices in a bowl; set aside. In another bowl, whisk together molasses and water; set aside. In a large bowl, with an electric mixer on low speed, beat butter and sugar until blended. Increase speed to high; beat until creamy, about 2 minutes. Reduce speed to low and add eggs, one at a time, beating well after each. Add flour mixture alternately with molasses mixture, beating until blended. Line the bottoms of three, 8" round cake pans with wax paper; grease and flour pans. Divide batter evenly among pans. Bake at 350 degrees for 25 to 30 minutes, until a toothpick tests clean. Cool in pans on wire racks for 10 minutes; turn cakes out onto racks and cool completely. Discard wax paper. Assemble cake with Buttercream Frosting (see left, page 114); chill until serving time.

Don't forget icy milk is perfect with gingerbread!
Serve it up in a new vintage-style milk bottle...
what a fun "remember when" memory.

Gingerbread Pudding Cake

Serves 6 to 8

1/4 c. butter, softened
1/4 c. sugar
1 egg white
1 t. vanilla extract
1/2 c. molasses
1 c. water
1-1/4 c. all-purpose flour
3/4 t. baking soda
1/4 t. salt

1/2 t. cinnamon
1/2 t. ground ginger
1/4 t. allspice
1/8 t. nutmeg
1/2 c. chopped pecans
6 T. brown sugar, packed
3/4 c. hot water
2/3 c. butter, melted
Garnish: whipped topping

In a large bowl, beat butter and sugar until light and fluffy. Beat in egg white and vanilla. In a separate small bowl, combine molasses and water. In another bowl, combine flour, baking soda, salt and spices. Gradually add flour mixture to butter mixture alternately with molasses mixture, beating well after each addition. Fold in pecans. Pour into a greased 3-quart slow cooker; sprinkle with brown sugar. Combine hot water and butter; pour over brown sugar. Do not stir. Cover and cook on high setting for 2 to 2-1/2 hours, until a toothpick inserted in the center tests clean. Turn off slow cooker; let stand for 15 minutes. Serve warm, scooped into bowls and garnished with whipped topping.

A game-day treat! Decorate a paper sack in team colors and fill with brownies. Fold the top over, punch 2 holes and slide a mini sports pennant through for a treat any sports fan will love.

Gingerbread Brownies

2-3/4 c. all-purpose flour
1 t. baking soda
1 t. salt
1 t. cinnamon
1 t. ground ginger
1/4 t. ground cloves
1-1/4 c. butter, softened

1-1/2 c. brown sugar, packed
1/2 c. sugar
2 eggs plus 1 egg yolk
1 t. vanilla extract
1/3 c. molasses
12-oz. pkg. white chocolate chips

In a bowl, whisk together flour, baking soda, salt and spices; set aside. In a separate large bowl, beat butter and sugars until creamy. Stir in eggs and egg yolk, one at a time; add vanilla and molasses. Stir in flour mixture until well mixed. Fold in chocolate chips. Spread batter in a greased or parchment paper-lined 15"x10" jelly-roll pan. Bake at 350 degrees for about 25 minutes, until set and golden. Cool completely in pan. Cut into 2-inch bars.

Sugar Cookie Dough

If cookies have been frozen ahead of time, it's a snap to make them taste fresh-baked in minutes. Place frozen cookies on a baking sheet and warm in a 300-degree oven for 3 to 5 minutes.

Wild Blueberry Gingerbread Squares

Makes 12 to 15 servings

1 tea bag
1 c. boiling water
2-1/2 c. all-purpose flour
1 c. sugar
1 t. baking soda
1 t. salt
1/2 t. ground cloves

1/2 t. ground ginger
1/2 t. cinnamon
1/2 c. molasses
2 eggs, beaten
1/2 c. oil
1 c. blueberries

Add tea bag to boiling water; let stand for 5 minutes. Mix together flour, sugar, baking soda, salt and spices in a large bowl. Discard tea bag; stir hot tea, molasses, eggs and oil into flour mixture. Gently fold in blueberries. Pour batter into a greased and floured 13"x9" baking pan. Bake at 350 degrees for 30 to 35 minutes. Cut into squares.

They went through the Raisin and Almond Gate,
into a wonderful little wood where gold and
silver fruit hung from the branches, tinsel sparkled
and there was a scent of oranges all around.
This was Christmas Wood.

—E.T.A. Hoffman, The Nutcracker

Grandma's Gingerbread Cake

Serves 12 to 15

3 c. all-purpose flour
1 t. baking soda
1 t. ground ginger
1 t. ground cloves
1 t. cinnamon

1 c. brown sugar, packed
1/2 c. margarine, melted
1 c. molasses
2 eggs
1 c. boiling water

In a large bowl, sift together flour, baking soda and spices; set aside. In another bowl, stir brown sugar into melted margarine. Add molasses and unbeaten eggs; beat well. Add flour mixture and boiling water to brown sugar mixture alternately in small amounts, beating thoroughly after each addition. Pour batter into a greased 13"x9" baking pan. Bake at 350 degrees for 25 minutes, or until a toothpick tests done. Cool; cut into squares.

Decorate cakes and trifles with a sparkling bunch of
sugared grapes...it's easier than it looks and so pretty
on a dessert buffet. Brush grapes with light corn syrup,
then sprinkle generously with sanding sugar and allow to dry.

Pumpkin Gingerbread Trifle

Makes 12 to 16 servings

14-1/2 oz. pkg. gingerbread
   cake mix
3.4-oz. pkg. instant vanilla
   pudding mix
2 c. milk
15-oz. can pumpkin

1/2 t. cinnamon
16-oz. container frozen whipped
   topping, thawed and divided
3 1.4-oz. chocolate-covered toffee
   candy bars, crushed

Prepare and bake cake mix according to package directions. Cool; tear or cut cake into large chunks and set aside. In a large bowl, whisk together dry pudding mix and milk for 2 minutes, until thickened; gently stir in pumpkin and cinnamon. In a clear glass trifle bowl, layer half each of cake chunks, pudding mixture and whipped topping. Repeat layers, ending with topping. Garnish with crushed candy bars. Cover and refrigerate at least 3 hours before serving.

INDEX

INDEX

Our Story

Back in 1984, we were next-door neighbors raising our families in the little town of Delaware, Ohio. Two moms with small children, we were looking for a way to do what we loved and stay home with the kids too. We had always shared a love of home cooking and making memories with family & friends and so, after many a conversation over the backyard fence, **Gooseberry Patch** was born.

We put together our first catalog at our kitchen tables, enlisting the help of our loved ones wherever we could. From that very first mailing, we found an immediate connection with many of our customers and it wasn't long before we began receiving letters, photos and recipes from these new friends. In 1992, we put together our very first cookbook, compiled from hundreds of these recipes and, the rest, as they say, is history.

Hard to believe it's been almost 40 years since those kitchen-table days! From that original little **Gooseberry Patch** family, we've grown to include an amazing group of creative folks who love cooking, decorating and creating as much as we do. Today, we're best known for our homestyle, family-friendly cookbooks, now recognized as national bestsellers.

One thing's for sure, we couldn't have done it without our friends all across the country. Each year, we're honored to turn thousands of your recipes into our collectible cookbooks. Our hope is that each book captures the stories and heart of all of you who have shared with us. Whether you've been with us since the beginning or are just discovering us, welcome to the **Gooseberry Patch** family!

Visit our website anytime
www.gooseberrypatch.com

Email

Jo Ann & Vickie

1·800·854·6673